SIMPLY COLOUR

50 CREATIVE IDEAS FOR IMPROVING YOUR HOME

LINDA BARKER
PHOTOGRAPHY BY LIZZIE ORME

SIMPLY
COLOUR

50 CREATIVE IDEAS FOR IMPROVING YOUR HOME

LINDA BARKER
PHOTOGRAPHY BY LIZZIE ORME

BCA

LONDON   NEW YORK   SYDNEY   TORONTO

For Jane, Jill, Sally and Ted

This edition published 1994 by
BCA by arrangement with

Anaya Publishers Ltd
Strode House, 44-50 Osnaburgh Street, London NW1 3ND

CN1955

Editor	Emma Callery
Design	Watermark Communications Group Ltd
Photographer	Lizzie Orme
Assisted by	Adam Robinson
Stylist	Linda Barker
Jacket Design	Watermark Communications Group Ltd

With thanks to Ted and Vicky for the location

Typeset in Great Britain by
Watermark Communications Group Ltd
Colour reproduction by HBM Print Pte, Singapore
Printed and bound in Malaysia by Times Offset Ltd

Contents

Introduction
7

INTRODUCTION

Colour is available to everyone and it comes in many guises each of which can be quick to use. Paint and fabric are the most obvious materials, but don't forget the less conventional forms of colour - dyes and crayons, beads and sequins, even plastic - each is just as colourful. I have a unique rag rug created by a brilliant designer who uses plastic shopping bags hooked in with more conventional fabrics to create a stunning effect. In this book, I too have used shopping bags - this time for painting with. And why not? You will discover some wonderful results and here I show you how to do it simply, step by step. In fact, painting with shopping bags isn't as messy as you may at first think, best of all there's no need to wash out the brushes. It has to be my favourite way of painting walls at the moment. It's good fun and, as I will show you in this book, you can achieve some glorious finishes using strong or soft, delicate colours.

We can also learn a lot by watching children at play, young children in particular. They instinctively collect odd assortments of coloured ribbons and scraps of fabric along with pretty beads and shiny plastic. I envy my small nieces' collections of shells and pebbles; their pieces of flotsam and jetsam hang from the kitchen ceiling and these treasures often find their way into my photographic work as a stylist. In a way, I have borrowed their sense of wonderment and excitement from these innocent collections and used this approach in my own work. It is the memory of rummaging through my mother's sewing box, finding coloured threads and scraps of pretty fabrics, that led me to create the ribbon and organza placemats in this book. Their sequins and glitter thread glint so attractively, appealing to both the sophisticated and the innocent. Along with these materials you will see that I also like to make good use of broken china and the odd coloured tile

to produce delicate mosaics on walls or simply to decorate an otherwise featureless surface such as a flower trough. The humble junk shop and car boot sales were regular hunting grounds for many of the materials I use in this book. Not even the grubby cardboard boxes tucked under the sales' counter escaped my eagle eye and more often than not these revealed a magpie's nest of glittering bits and pieces.

It can be very refreshing to see odd assortments of glass and china that you thought would never go together somehow complementing each other brilliantly. Take a rusty old baking tray with some crystal candelabra drops and immediately a source of inspiration is found. Observe how a neglected brass candlestick starts to oxidize and turn green with verdigris; all of these are such fabulous colours, found quite naturally in everyday life. In this book I'll show you how to accelerate the natural verdigris process using special products that mean you don't have to wait ten years for Mother Nature to take its effect.

Accidentally stumbling upon materials that work brilliantly together can also work for colours. Quite often, colours of the same density vie for attention if they are put together and your eye becomes confused, darting between the two, making you feel uneasy. However, on a small scale, vibrant orange and lime green - such as those used on my gerbera bowl - produce an exciting explosion of colour. Rules are there to be broken, experiment with colour by painting on to scraps of paper and build up a small collage to see how different colours work together. Use the same approach for fabrics, beads and ribbons, assembling all kinds of bits and pieces; take some pieces out, add more of another colour. In this way you will develop a palette of colours that are particular to your own tastes and to no one else's. I've always loved orange curtains in my lilac room anyhow!

There are so many ordinary, everyday products and materials that can be used creatively, too. Take conventional powder filler, normally associated with boring jobs such as filling the holes in your walls or cracked skirting boards - you probably have an old packet at the back of your cupboard. Well don't throw it out because it takes on a whole new lease of life when mixed with emulsion paint. It produces the most wondrous gooey mess that can be piped, like icing, around a picture frame and it then dries rock hard. Or spread it over plastic flower vases, together with coils of string, to transform ugly pieces of utility plastic into *objets d'art*; well almost. Tin cans and dusty old biscuit tins don't escape the paintbrush either and if you thought the photocopier was for the office then think again. I bet you never imagined covering your walls with colour photocopies such as those featured here in the kitchen on page 64.

Above all else I want you to enjoy colouring your home be it in a small way by adding a coloured lampshade or a large way by colourwashing your walls, and I hope I can inspire you to be adventurous in your decoration.

Equipment

A magpie's collection of bits and pieces is all you really need to get going and a place to work - there's nothing quite as infuriating as having to clear away all your carefully arranged mosaic pieces ready for sticking just as you're getting going. A shed at the bottom of the garden would be fine if you can shut the door and be left alone to get on with it. Unfortunately, gardens are as expensive as houses in London, where I work, so that romantic concept unhappily doesn't apply to me. However, I have a wonderful studio with drawers full of shells and ribbons, vibrant squares of felt, paint, feathers, beads and coloured papers. Nevertheless, a table top is perfectly alright so long as you can spread your materials out in front of you.

Paint charts Invariably we have to rely on these tiny charts when choosing our wall colours, a very difficult thing to do. The trick is to take the paint chart into daylight if possible and preferably with a small swatch of the fabric that may be in the room. Hold the square at arms' length and squint at it to see the effect of the colour.

Paints I generally try to use water-based paints; not only are they kinder to the environment but they are simple to use and it is easy to wash your hands and brushes clean once the job is finished. Specialist paints such as ceramic and glass paints are available from good art supply shops or craft outlets. Always check the labels on these products to ensure that the piece of glass or china that is to be painted can be used afterwards or whether the painted objects are only for decoration. Gouache colour is an artist quality paint and it can be used thinly with lots of water to create a delicate wash or thickly to create a solid area of colour such as on the carrot image I used for the kitchen wall decoration.

Brushes For the painted projects you will need a selection of good brushes in several widths. You will need small brushes for craft projects and larger ones for some of the wall treatments - it is always good to pick up special offer multi-packs but be aware of the cheap and nasties. They may look alright inside the packaging but as soon as you start to paint they deposit stray hairs every second or third brush stroke, which becomes very irritating. When you've finished a particular project, wash brushes religiously. I always try to use water-based paints and use lots of warm soapy water at first and then rinse thoroughly, smoothing the hairs flat. Hang the bristles over the edge of a worktop to let the air flow around them so that they can dry thoroughly.

Art brushes are also available in many shapes and forms and although the initial investment may be high these should last a long time provided you care for them. I rarely use very fine brushes except for particularly detailed work. Hog hair brushes are perfect for the projects outlined in this book.

Inexpensive paste brushes are a good investment as they save your best brushes from ending up in the glue pot.

Varnishing requires a special flat brush available from art shops and good decorating shops and should only be used for varnishing, nothing else. I try to use water-based acrylic varnish whenever possible as the brushes can be quickly washed out in water.

Paint palettes and china saucers These are very convenient for mixing small quantities of paint or holding tiny amounts of glue and it is useful to have a stack of these to hand. Use your old ones, chipped ones or the hideous pink and purple ones that were part of a bargain gift set that your elderly aunt gave you for Christmas. Anything that saves the Royal Doulton.

Wax crayons Steal your children's colours to tint your homemade candles.

Sewing machines vary greatly, but the majority of the projects can be done using a straight stitch on any machine. A couple of projects use an embroidery stitch which your machine may or may not have. If it does, and you haven't used it before then I hope you will be tempted to do so as it is so simple to make the upholstery fringing which can cost a fortune in the shops. For those machines without this facility, I have always outlined an alternative that a basic machine will be able to cope with.

Pins and needles The fabric projects in this book range from small hand-stitched napkin rings, to more elaborate curtain treatments requiring a sewing machine of some kind, be it hand cranked or high tech. The enormous variety of pins and needles that are available amazes me, ranging as they do from semi-circular upholstery needles to the finest wedding dress pins. All that is required for these projects are the common dressmaker's pins and a packet of assorted household needles, available nationwide. I must confess, however, to being tempted into purchasing the odd wheel of pretty glass headed pins.

Fabrics The project that you are working on determines the type of fabric that is needed, and I always recommend a certain fabric for any one project. It is obviously sensible to use a washable fabric whenever you can, particularly on, say, a tablecloth or for some napkins. If more than one fabric is to be used for one project and you are buying the fabrics new, study the washing labels carefully, to ensure they are compatible for washing and that the colours are fast.

Fabric dyes These are sold in several forms: hot or cold water dyes, hand or machine dyes. I always try to dye fabric in a washing machine as it ensures an evenness of colour and is very convenient to use. Whichever dye you choose to work with, always read the manufacturer's instructions carefully first.

Bondaweb is a soft material that bonds fabric to fabric once it is pressed with a hot iron. This quality makes it ideal for appliqué and you will find it invaluable if you want to follow my instructions for the ribbon and organza placemats.

Ribbons and organza are materials that are always part of my basic work kit. These are generally bought as oddments or remnants and I am constantly adding to this supply: if I see a pretty ribbon, I may just buy it for my ever-growing collection, with the hope of it being just the thing for a future project. Car boot sales are excellent places for buying tied-up bundles of maybe six or seven different ribbons, of which several will be alright but one or even two will be particularly attractive.

Sequins, beads and buttons Buy these on a whim and store them in clean jam jars, on display if possible, to inspire new ideas.

Coloured papers and wrapping papers are lovely to have a supply of if you have the space to store them, and can then be purchased whenever you see one you particularly like the design of.

Filler and wallpaper paste Whether you are creating craft pieces of generally improving your home, general hardware supplies such as these are useful to have around. Once you discover my filler

and emulsion paint mixture, though, you may want to increase your supply.

Flotsam and jetsam What I would give to live near a beach! Shells and pebbles are all beautiful things to have to hand. At the moment I can't get enough driftwood or those glorious pieces of frosted glass that start life as broken bottles and the sea turns into little jewels. Feathers and bits of sheep's wool pulled from barbed wire on walks in the countryside, all these things are squirrelled away in my workshop awaiting transformation. Any other materials that are not mentioned should be familiar to most people but you will find an easy-to-follow ingredients list at the start of each project that you can quickly run through and check off before you begin.

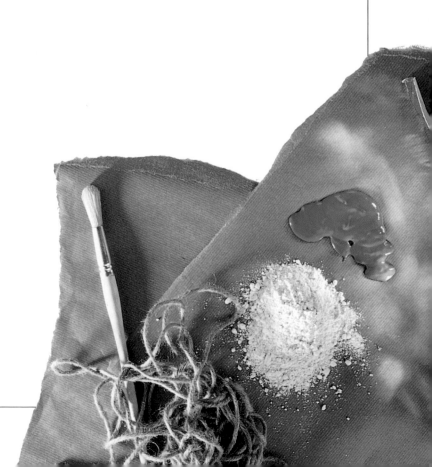

CHAPTER 1

DECORATIVE COLOURS

The dining room was my starting point for many of the colourful designs in this chapter. The pine table didn't stand a chance, neither did anything else come to that matter - and my windows went through their third transformation this year!

Most of the projects in this chapter use elementary skills that most of us probably learnt as children. Also, practically everything can be made with very little money, a bit of effort, a bit of ingenuity and, for many of the designs, you may have the materials at home already.

Don't feel restricted to applying the techniques just to the surfaces I have suggested: the brightly coloured flower napkin rings are eye-catching on a small scale, but how about sewing seven or eight flowers on to a curtain tieback? Don't be afraid to experiment, and enjoy working with the colour in as many ways as you can think of.

Sunburst
Sheer Drapes

Dying muslin is quick and easy in a washing machine and the choice of colours are infinitely more interesting than having to use either white or cream muslin. The sunburst panels can be attached quickly using eyelets.

MATERIALS

tape measure

cotton muslin

fabric dye

salt

sewing machine

thread

scissors

brown paper

pencil

canvas

self-adhesive felt

eyelets

hammer

ribbon

Hints

Enlarge the sunburst motif on this page on a photocopier to a 10cm/4in diameter. Then cut out the outline and use as a template. If you use ordinary felt, use a straight stitch on the sewing machine to sew the motif on to the panel.

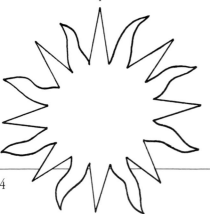

1 Use the tape measure to calculate the amount of muslin you will need to cover your window. Allow 2.5cm/1in at the top and bottom for turnings and 7.5cm/3in at each edge for the zigzag detail. Add 30cm/12in to each drop for the sunburst panels. Dye according to the instructions.

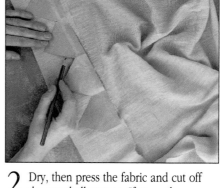

2 Dry, then press the fabric and cut off the panel allowance. If more than one drop is used, stitch these pieces together. Turn over the seam allowances and stitch. Using overlapping corners of paper, create a zigzag template for the curtain edge and mark along the curtain edges using a pencil.

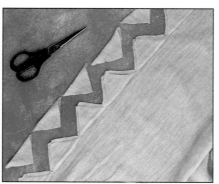

3 Stitch along the pencil zigzag line and then cut off the excess fabric using sharp scissors. Press, turning the excess fabric on the zigzags to the wrong side. To make this easier, you will need to snip the top off each zigzag point and snip into each zigzag bottom almost to the line of stitching.

4 For each width of fabric used, cut the extra piece of muslin into five 15 x 25cm/6 x 10in panels. Turn under the smallest seam allowance on all four sides to finish. Cut canvas panels 2.5cm/1in wider all around, fray three sides to a depth of 2.5cm/1in, turn under the top allowance and place the muslin panel on top. Cut the sun from the felt and glue in place.

5 Position the panels along the top edge of the curtain, spacing them out evenly so they have equal gaps between. Secure each panel on to the curtain with two eyelets using the hammer and simple assembly tool sold with the eyelets. Use ribbon to secure the curtain to the rail.

Leafy Table Top

Junk shops and car boot sales are great places for finding old tables or pieces of furniture that can be transformed with a touch of colour in this way. A lot of the hard preparation work can be done using an electric sander if you have one.

MATERIALS

table

sander and sandpaper
(coarse, medium and fine grades)

thin cardboard

craft knife

old paintbrush

masking fluid

paintbrushes

green emulsion paint

artist's paintbrush

pink acrylic paint

grey acrylic paint

furniture wax

Hints

Masking fluid is very simple to use. It dries to a rubbery finish which can then be painted over and later peeled off. Wash the brush in warm soapy water regularly during the masking-off process to prevent a build-up of the fluid which otherwise would soon clog up your brush. The decorative detail looks best on the top of the table. Paint the table base plain, using green emulsion paint.

1 Prepare the table, stripping off any traces of old varnish or paint. Trace off our leaf on to thin cardboard and use the craft knife to cut carefully around the outline to get your stencil. Hold the stencil in place and use the old paintbrush to paint masking fluid through the stencil. Repeat across the table top, creating an informal pattern of tumbling leaves.

2 Use a household paintbrush to paint on the green emulsion paint; don't worry about trying to create a flawless finish as the surface of the table will later be distressed. Also, it doesn't matter if paint is brushed over the dried masking fluid as you can still see where the leaves are underneath.

3 When the emulsion layer is quite dry, peel off the masking fluid. You may need to start the process by rubbing the top of the surface with your finger which soon makes the rubber solution wrinkle. Sand the whole table using medium then fine grade sandpaper to distress the finish.

4 Use a fairly broad artist's paintbrush to paint boldly in thick strokes of pink acrylic paint on the leaves and dash in four quick strokes using the grey paint for the veined leaf detail. When this painting is quite dry, seal and protect the whole surface with a layer of antique wax.

17

Felt Notice Board

It seems to me that it is impossible to buy anything vaguely connected to the office in anything other than black, white or shades of grey. But most homes these days have a notice board of some description - even if it's only to pin the shopping list to - so customize your own with brightly coloured felt.

MATERIALS

notice board

coloured felt

scissors

PVA adhesive

glue brush

ribbon

ruler

decorative headed tacks

stapler (optional)

emulsion paint

paintbrush

masking tape or panel pins

Hints

Use a contrasting ribbon for the most dramatic effect or criss-cross lots of different coloured ribbons.

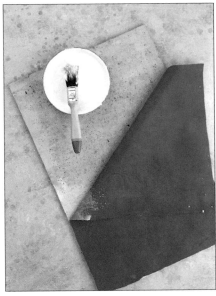

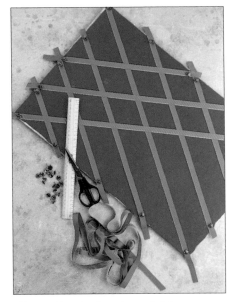

1 Carefully remove the frame from the notice board by stripping off the back tape or removing the fastenings. If these can be re-used, keep them on one side and use again when reassembling. Strip the old material covering from the board and glue down a piece of felt cut to the same size, using PVA adhesive.

2 Position the first piece of ribbon diagonally across the board and secure the ends with tacks. Use a ruler to position three parallel rows of ribbon on each side of this first one, keeping the distance between ribbons equal. Secure as before, then repeat across the other diagonal to form a diamond pattern.

3 Push tacks through the ribbons at the points where the ribbons cross. Remove the tacks from the outer edge and staple or glue these outer ribbons down. Use emulsion to paint the frame and wait for it to dry before reassembling. Secure the board to the frame using tape or panel pins.

Ribbon
Picture Mount

Greetings cards are so attractive
that it seems a shame to throw
them away once the birthday or
festive occasion has passed.
With this simple ribbonwork
mount, the prettiest cards can
be displayed like pictures.

MATERIALS

greetings card

thin cardboard

ruler

pencil

craft knife

selection of ribbons

PVA adhesive

glue brush

masking tape

picture frame (if required)

Hints

Cut your cardboard for the mount to fit
inside a plain picture frame and then paint
it to match one of the coloured ribbons.
Alternatively, cut the mount and then glue
another piece of cardboard behind it for the
backing and make a triangular piece of
cardboard to form a support.

1 Determine the size of your mount by measuring inside a picture frame or by simply deciding where you are going to display the picture and making the frame to suit your own requirements (see Hints, left). Using the craft knife, cut a window in the mount to display the card.

2 Cut pieces of ribbon to form horizontal stripes across the cardboard. Fold the ends of the ribbons on to the back of the mount and glue down. Use any combination of coloured ribbons - I think they look best if there isn't a regular pattern.

3 Thread more lengths of ribbon vertically through the horizontal bands, threading over one piece, then under the next until a pleasing pattern is reached. Leave thin, then wide, gaps between ribbons. Secure the ribbons at the back as before. As suggested in Step 1, tape the card in place in a frame, or display.

Tissue Lampshade

This is a pretty shade that is designed for use with a low-wattage bulb. Several colours of tissue paper are built up on top of each other, trapping sequins between the layers for a pretty effect when the light is switched on.

MATERIALS

candle lampshade fitting

plastic backing paper

marker pen

ruler

2 or 3 colours of tissue paper

wallpaper paste

sequins

scissors

PVA adhesive

glue brush

Hints

Build up the layers of tissue randomly: don't be afraid to have only one or two thicknesses in some areas and four or five thicknesses in other places. This is often prettier when the light is switched on.

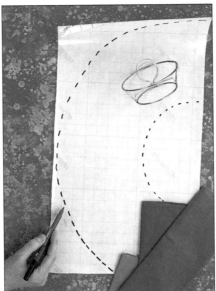

1 Place the candle lampshade on the plastic backing, aligning a marked point on the edge of the smallest wire ring with the edge of the plastic. Roll the shade, adding frequent small lines to the plastic, until the marked point has been reached again and complete the arc with the marker pen. Set the ruler against the arc and mark the depth of the shade.

2 Tear long strips of coloured tissue paper and lay these between the two arcs using wallpaper paste. Allow the strips to overlap the marked lines. Place a few sequins between the layers.

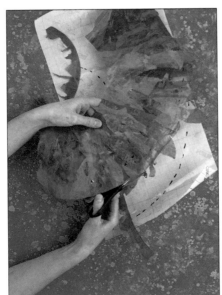

3 Once the area has been covered with tissue layers, leave it to dry thoroughly, preferably overnight. Once dry it can easily be removed from the plastic backing. The marker pen will have made a visible line on the tissue to cut along with a pair of scissors.

4 Fold the shade and overlap the edges by 2.5cm/1in using PVA adhesive to secure the ends firmly. Several more sequins may also be stuck on at this stage. The base of the shade may be scalloped using scissors or left plain, then simply placed over the candle shade.

Organza and Ribbon Placemats

These placemats will add a touch of elegance to any table setting. The trapped sequins and glitter thread are particularly attractive and you can find them in any good haberdashery department.

MATERIALS

coloured organza

Bondaweb fabric

iron and ironing board

paper

scissors

selection of ribbons, including some organza ribbon

sequins

cotton cloth

glitter thread

sewing machine

Hints

Bondaweb fuses the threaded ribbons securely to the organza. If Bondaweb is not available, then a little fabric glue could be spread thinly on the right side of the organza and the threaded ribbons pressed on to it. Leave it to dry before sewing.

1 Cut a piece of organza to the required size of the placemat plus 2.5cm/1in all around. Using a cool iron, fuse the Bondaweb to one side of the organza. Trim to the same size as the organza. Keep the iron on a cool setting for the whole project or you will melt the delicate organza.

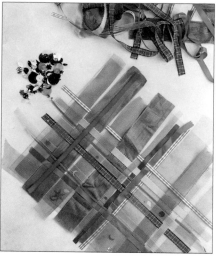

2 Cut a piece of paper to the size of your placemat and build the ribbonwork over this. Leaving spaces between the ribbons, lay the horizontal ribbons first and then thread the vertical ribbons over and under them to create a latticework pattern. Trap sequins between the delicate organza ribbons.

3 Use the paper to lift the ribbonwork on to the ironing board. Remove the backing paper from the fused Bondaweb and place the bonded organza, matt side down, on top of the ribbons. Cover with the damp cotton cloth and iron to secure the ribbons to the organza.

4 Use the glitter thread and a straight stitch on your sewing machine to sew occasional horizontal and vertical lines across the placemat to strengthen the mat and to trap the sequins. Finish the edges with a more solid line of decorative machine embroidery (if you have this facility on your machine), or use a close zigzag stitch. Trim any loose threads.

Flower Napkin Rings

With these wonderful napkin rings, meal times need never be boring.

MATERIALS

paper

pencil

scissors

coloured felt

self-covered buttons

thin cardboard

gingham

sewing machine

thread

needle

Hints

Use a photocopier to enlarge the flower outlines from this page to a suitable size.

1 Enlarge the flower outlines (see Hints, left) and cut each one from the paper to use as templates. Cut out as many felt flowers as you require (one per napkin ring). Separate the same number of uncovered buttons and place a circle of felt over one part, pushing the edge of the felt on to the gripper teeth. Reassemble the two halves to form each button.

2 Cut rectangles of 5 x 20cm/2 x 8in from the cardboard to form the napkin rings and cut pieces of gingham to cover the rings, adding a 2.5cm/1in allowance on each side for the seams. Turn a small allowance under with a straight stitch on the sewing machine then hand sew the fabric allowances together around the cardboard.

3 Place a covered button on top of a felt flower and stitch these two pieces to the centre of the fabric-covered cardboard, sewing through all the thicknesses. Repeat for all the napkin rings and finally hand stitch the ring closed.

Sand-cast Candles

Colour the melted wax with wax crayons; the more crayons you add, the stronger will be the colour of the candle. A quantity of 450g/1lb of wax will make three or four small candles or one large one.

MATERIALS

plastic bowl or bucket

damp sand

starfish or shells

spray bottle

candle wax

wax crayons

tin can or old pan

large pan

oven mitt

old plastic glove

candle wick

plastic jug

scissors

Hints

If you don't have anything suitable for the mould, simply dig a hole with your hand. For pretty decoration, seashells can then be pressed into the sides of the hole with the shells' right sides facing the sand.

1 Fill the plastic bowl with damp sand and press your starfish or shells into this. Remove the object to reveal the impression in the sand. If you have a poor impression, dampen the sand again and repeat.

2 Spray the impression with water to prevent the sand crumbling. Melt the wax and crayons over the stove in a tin can or an old pan set over another pan of water, continually stirring.

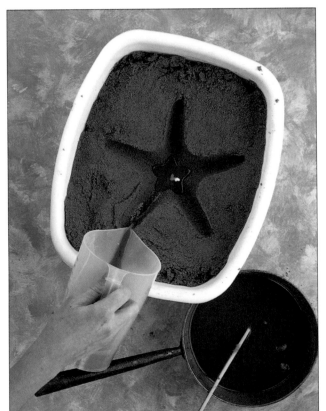

3 Wearing the old plastic glove, dip a piece of wick 10cm/4in longer than your candle into the wax and allow to cool. Still wearing the glove, push the wick into the sand hole and hold it straight while you carefully pour the melted wax from the plastic jug into the mould in a steady stream. Hold the wick straight until the wax cools and it can support itself; then leave the candle to set for a few hours until it is hard. Dig it out of the sand, trim the wick and dust off any loose sand: it is part of the attraction if a little sand sticks to the surface of the wax.

Painted Ceramics

These thermohardening ceramic colours can be purchased in lots of different hues so you can easily transform your plain china into a bright tartan plaid, just as I did here.

MATERIALS

chinagraph marker pencil

plain white ceramics

ruler (optional)

thermohardening ceramic paints

paintbrushes

palette

Hints

Let each colour dry thoroughly before painting on the next one otherwise the colours tend to merge together and become dirty.

1 Use a chinagraph marker to mark on a noughts and crosses-type grid across the flat surface of the china. You could use a ruler to determine the distance between the lines but I favour slight fluctuations in the size of each square to give a more handcrafted quality.

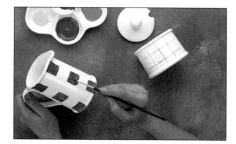

2 Paint the first square using a little ceramic paint. Paint the edges of the square first, then fill it in. Don't worry about letting the brush marks show in the paint - I feel that this is all part of the charm. Continue painting with this colour, building up a pattern as I have done.

3 Apply the second colour in the same way. Continue around the jug as I have done, slowly building up the checked pattern. Try to keep the colours quite thin as the top colour will overlap these and will not dry successfully if the paint is too thick.

4 Use a fine brush and a steady hand to paint in the thin lines that form the tartan finish. Occasionally the paint may blob or you may run out of paint,but don't worry about this. Allow the paint to dry thoroughly before baking the china in the oven according to the instructions on the paint.

Mosaic Wine Coasters

At last I have found a use for all those brightly coloured odd tiles I collected from car boot sales, but since most tile suppliers are happy to sell odd tiles, you can soon build up an eclectic assortment.

MATERIALS

paper

pencil

hardboard

fret saw

sandpaper (fine grade)

tile adhesive/grout

spreader

coloured tiles

hammer

cotton cloth

felt

PVA adhesive

glue brush

Hints

Place each tile between several thicknesses of newspaper and give it a few sharp taps with a hammer to break it into tiny mosaic pieces.

1 Enlarge the template from this page on a photocopier to a suitable size. Alternatively, draw your own pattern on paper using the base of a wine glass as a size guide. Cut this shape from the paper and use it as a template to draw on the hardboard.

2 Cut around each shape carefully using a fret saw and use a small piece of fine-grade sandpaper to smooth any uneven edges. Use the spreader to skim a thin layer of tile adhesive/grout over the top surface of the coaster, trying to maintain an even thickness.

3 Break the tiles into small pieces (see Hints, left) and build up a pattern on the coaster starting in the centre and working outwards. On some coasters I have followed the shape of the coaster when making the pattern and on others I have started with a daisy shape and filled the mosaic pieces around this.

4 Leave the mosaic to set, then apply a thick layer of tile adhesive/grout over the whole coaster, pushing it between the mosaic pieces and around the edges of the coaster. Scrape off the excess grout and wipe the surface clear with a damp cloth before the adhesive/grout dries. Cut a felt backing and glue it to the bottom.

Painted Wine Glasses

These ordinary wine glasses are given a colourful treatment using glass paints which dry to a water-resistant finish. Although they are reasonably hard wearing don't attempt to put them in the dishwasher.

MATERIALS

glasses

tube of black glass relief paint

glass paints

fine paintbrushes

palette for mixing paint

scissors

Hints

Most glass paints are transparent. But if you prefer the opaque qualities I have used here, simply mix a little white glass paint with the transparent colour.

1 Place the glass to be decorated over one of the motifs on this page (enlarge the motif on a photocopier if necessary), close one eye and outline the image using the black relief paint directly on to the glass. It only works with one eye closed! Try to squeeze the tube evenly so the outline is consistent - you may want to practise on paper first.

2 Paint the glass in as many colours as you like. I used three separate colours for this glass, but you could easily use more colours or just one if you prefer. I would prefer several glasses, each painted in a different way, but it's up to you. Allow each colour to dry before using the next.

3 Paint inside the relief area using a contrasting colour so that the design has more impact (all glass colours can be mixed to produce different colours if required). Leave to dry overnight so they become rock hard.

4 When the glass is quite dry, etch into the painted glass with a closed pair of scissors. I have etched small scrolls into the glass rim and a zigzag pattern around the base, but vary your patterns on each glass. The glasses should only be washed by hand.

Spray-painted Lampshade

Use a spray paint that is sympathetic to the fabric of your lampshade: some sprays will cover most surfaces including glass, plastic, even metal.

MATERIALS

lamp

cloth tape measure

self-adhesive plastic

marker pen

scissors

spray paint

Hints

Hold the lowest part of the lampshade nearest to the spray-paint nozzle. This part will then receive the full blast of paint and the top of the lamp will receive the least. The result is a finely graduated paint finish.

1 Remove the shade from the lamp and use the tape measure to determine the circumference of the shade where you wish the pattern to be. My wavy line runs closer to the base of the shade than the top as the darker shading emphasizes the wave more clearly.

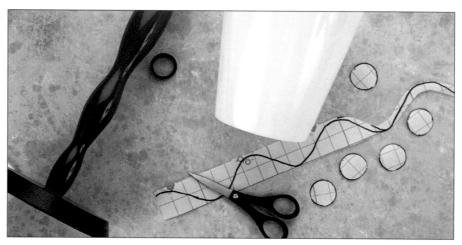

2 Cut a rectangle from the self-adhesive plastic using the circumference as the length and the depth of the wave as the width. Draw a wavy line so that it starts and finishes at the top of a crest to maintain a continuous pattern around the lamp. Cut enough small circles so that one fits beneath each wave.

3 Cut the wave from the plastic to a width of 1cm/2.5in. Remove the backing paper and glue it smoothly on to the lampshade ensuring that it is level all the way around. Position the dots. Spray (see Hints, left), then leave to dry before removing the plastic.

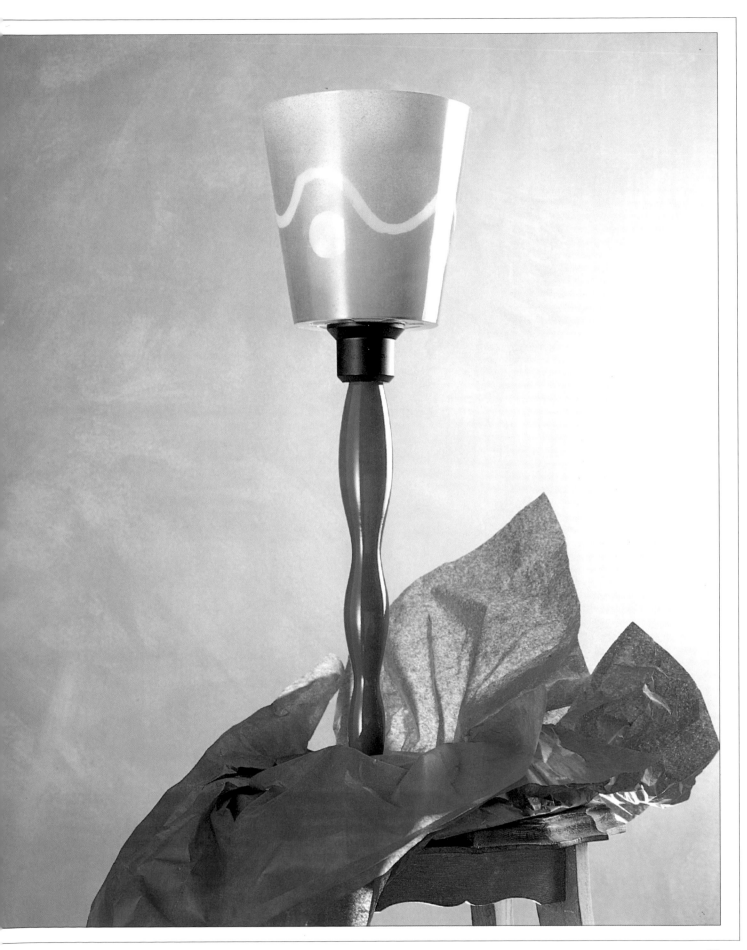

Dining Room Wall Treatment

A simple wall wash is gloriously uncomplicated to achieve and looks fabulous on even or uneven walls alike. If you're bored with the existing colour, a wash with diluted colour will soften and add character to a flat colour. It is also a perfect backdrop for stencilling.

MATERIALS

emulsion paint in base colour

paintbrush

white emulsion paint or
paler version of existing top colour

plastic container

cellulose sponge

household brush

Hints

Rather than trying to get the paint into the corners using the sponge, use a little of the diluted wash on the ends of a dry brush and rub this into the corners, brushing out the marks until the paint dries.

1 If you are starting the paint finish from the beginning, paint the walls with two good coats of the base colour. If you have coloured walls that are going to be treated to a wall wash, ensure the walls are cleaned with warm soapy water.

2 Mix together an equal quantity of coloured base colour with white emulsion, then double this volume with water and mix together well to produce a thin paint. If you are using a paler version of the top coat of an existing colour, mix this with an equal amount of water.

3 Cut the sponge in half and dip one half into the wash. Use a scrubbing motion all over the walls to transfer the paint, working your sponge across the still wet surface until it dries. This not only catches drips, it softens and clouds the painted surface too. Continue working in one area at a time, but do not allow the leading edge to dry.

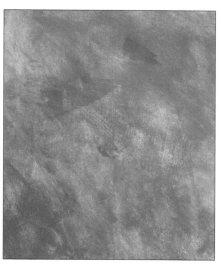

4 Mix a darker top colour for the final wash. Use the other half of the sponge and repeat the process as in the previous step. Build up a cloudy layer of colour adding more paint until you are satisfied with the result.

CHAPTER 2

A SPLASH OF COLOUR

Brightly coloured kitchens get my vote every time and cooking in this Mediterranean-style environment inspires my creativity. If the carrots aren't quite to your taste, you'll find lots of other images in magazines or gardening publications that you could use as alternatives. How about a chicken, a flower or a topiary tree? Take your inspiration from books, designer showrooms and magazines .

As in Chapter 1, there is no need to spend a fortune on any of the projects here. You can recycle aluminium cans to provide the basis of decoration for the storage box and use it either to keep letters and trinkets inside or as a stylish tidy box for odds and ends. Make an ordinary little piece of furniture into a spectacular egg cupboard, or spice up a spice rack with a clever paint finish.

Kitchen Stool

These old-fashioned style stools can be purchased new or you might find them second-hand. They are usually brown or beige with natural cane or woven seats: nothing like the latticed checks that I have used here and, of course, the framework had to be painted bright blue to match.

MATERIALS

stool

2 colours of gingham

scissors

sewing machine

thread

staple gun

oil-based paint

paintbrush

Hints

Carpet tacks can be used instead of a staple gun to secure the woven strips, use two tacks at each end for extra security.

1 If possible, take the stool apart and remove all the old seat coverings from the seat base. Cut 7.5cm/3in-wide strips from the gingham, cutting each strip to a length that will cover the seat and provide enough allowance to be stapled underneath. Sew a small seam down the sides of each strip.

2 Cover across the seat base with horizontal strips of fabric. Pull each strip as tight as possible and secure with staples underneath the base so they cannot be seen. Don't worry about pattern matching as this adds to the final effect.

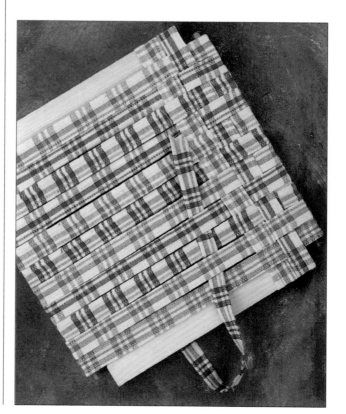

3 Thread the vertical strips through the horizontal bands, following a regular pattern of over one band then under the next. Alternate this procedure for each strip to create a tight lattice effect. Push each band close to its neighbour for a strong structure. Trim the strips underneath the base, paint the stool and reassemble.

String Vase

This wonderful vase started life as two plain plastic containers. I stuck them together and decorated them with a gooey mixture of paint and filler with the odd length of string thrown in.

MATERIALS

2 plastic containers

strong adhesive (epoxy resin)

filler

blue emulsion paint

old paintbrush

Hints

I think this spiral design looks good wrapped around the vase but you could shape the string into any number of different formations, or experiment with bands that are closer together or further apart.

1 Use a strong glue to secure the bases of the containers together and give them a good tug once they are dry to make sure they are going to stay stuck. Mix the filler with enough emulsion paint to give you a thick paste; you may need to add a little water as emulsion paints and fillers vary in consistency.

2 Cover the first 25cm/10in of string with some of the paste - be prepared to get completely messy at this stage. Lay the end of the string along the edge of one container and begin to bind it around the containers, painting on more paste as needed.

3 Continue spiralling the string around and take care to progress as neatly as possible over the point at which the containers join. The paste takes a little time to harden so there is time to remove the string and start again if necessary. Paint paste 2.5cm/1in inside the top rim and then leave to dry.

Egg Cupboard

The quality of this coloured photocopy is so good you would have to look twice to realize that it's not a high quality print. It's such a very clever way of turning a simple little cupboard into something out of the ordinary.

MATERIALS

glass-fronted cupboard	tin snips
chicken photograph	brown gummed tape
scissors	panel pins (optional)
hardboard	hammer (optional)
saw	oil-based paint or emulsion paint
chicken wire	paintbrush

Hints

Any simple glass-fronted cupboard can be given this treatment. The wooden shelves inside have been drilled at regular intervals using a 7.5cm/3in drill bit which provide just the right support for the eggs. It could also be used to display a collection of decorative eggs.

1 Select your favourite photograph of a chicken. If, like my photograph, the top of the print is dark, cut it away and replace with the lighter parts from another photograph to make a montage. Place it on a colour photocopier and enlarge it so that you have a print to fit the cupboard panel.

2 Cut the hardboard to the same size as the glass panel and glue the print on to the front. Snip out a piece of chicken wire using the hardboard as a template and lay it inside the glass door.

3 Place the hardboard over the chicken wire, ensuring the chicken is the right way up. Secure the panel to the door using gummed tape, and panel pins if necessary. If you need to use panel pins be careful not to break the glass: lay the cupboard on a padded surface and tap the pins in at an angle.

4 If, like this one, the cupboard has been varnished you will need to paint the frame using oil-based paint. If not, you will be able to use emulsion or water-based paints. Put in the wooden shelves and hang the cupboard securely on the wall.

Spice Rack

Distressed colour allows one colour to show through another and often works best when two contrasting colours are used together, as on this spice rack.

MATERIALS

plain spice rack

pink emulsion paint

blue emulsion paint

small paintbrushes

sandpaper (medium grade)

Hints

On larger objects you will find it easier to remove the top layer of emulsion paint from its base coat if you rub some hard wax between the layers.

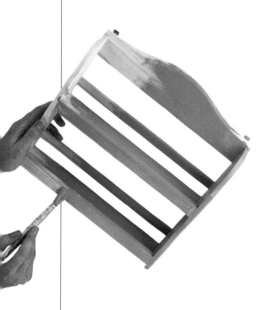

1 Using pink emulsion and a small paintbrush to reach the corners, paint a base coat on to the spice rack. When this is dry, cover with a layer of the blue top coat. You needn't worry about applying this coat with the same careful coverage as for the first colour since most of it will be removed.

2 When the blue emulsion layer is quite dry, start to wear away the top surface with the sandpaper. It will be more interesting if you rub certain areas more than others and in some places the natural wood could even show through.

Appliqué Tablecloth

Use the boldest colours that you can find in your fabric department and don't necessarily be persuaded to use green for the leaves: I found blue and orange combine perfectly.

MATERIALS

scissors

fabric for leaves (blue)

chalk

Bondaweb

iron and ironing board

fabric for tablecloth (orange)

sewing machine

thread

Hints

Bondaweb makes appliqué incredibly simple as it secures the motif to the cloth and doesn't move until it is firmly stitched. If it isn't available you will have to resort to the labour-intensive method of pinning the leaf to the fabric with lots and lots of pins and hoping it doesn't shift as you machine or hand stitch it in place.

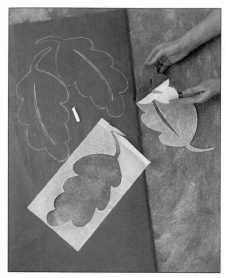 

1 Use the enlargement facility on a photocopier to increase the leaves on this page to a size that fits your table. Be bold and go for dramatic, oversized leaves. Cut the leaf from the paper and use it as a template: position it on to the right side of the blue cloth and draw around its edge with chalk. Place a sheet of Bondaweb on to the wrong side, iron over it and then cut out the motif.

2 Place the blue fabric on top of the table to be covered and draw a freehand curve to represent the stem from which the leaves are falling. Cut this from the cloth, maintaining an even width of approximately 2.5cm/1in. Secure Bondaweb to the wrong side of the stalk. Iron the leaves and stalk on to the tablecloth fabric.

3 Use a close zigzag stitch on the machine to sew around the leaves and the stalk. Feed the fabric slowly under the sewing foot as the bends and twists on the leaves are tricky to negotiate at speed. If your sewing machine has one, finish the hem around the cloth with a decorative embroidery stitch, or use a zigzag.

Sunflower
Plant Pots

The humble terracotta plant pot
comes out of the garden shed.

MATERIALS

plant pots

white emulsion paint

paintbrush

blue emulsion paint

plastic container

cotton cloth

wrapping paper

scissors

PVA adhesive

glue brush

acrylic varnish

Hints

Any flowery wrapping paper or pictures
cut from magazines or seed catalogues could
be used to decorate these pots.

1 Paint the outside of each flower pot with a layer of white emulsion paint. Mix one part blue emulsion paint with one part water in the plastic container to make a diluted solution. When the white emulsion is dry paint this solution over the pot.

2 While the paint is still wet, remove some of the blue paint from the surface of the pot with a damp cotton cloth to reveal some of the white paint underneath. Keep turning the cloth over as the paint builds up and rinse it out occasionally.

3 Cut flower motifs from the wrapping paper. These sunflowers are quite intricate, but it is worthwhile spending time cutting away all the background colour. Glue the flowers on the flat surface of the pot and allow to dry before painting with acrylic varnish for protection.

Painted Tinware

These attractive tins started life as ordinary biscuit tins that are usually thrown out with the rubbish once the contents have been eaten.

MATERIALS

old tin

car spray paint

star template

masking tape

small piece of wood

hammer

nail

enamel paint

paintbrush

Hints

Always slide a piece of wood underneath the area to be punched and support it on a solid surface such as a table or workbench. Otherwise you'll find the whole panel will be punched in.

1 Remove any labels from the tin and wash with warm soapy water. Spray the outer surfaces of the tin with car spray paint. You will find this easier if you protect the surrounding area with newspaper as the spray paint particles get everywhere. Leave the tin for 10 minutes to dry thoroughly.

2 Enlarge the template on this page using a photocopier until you have a size that fits your tin, or draw your own heart or flower shapes. Fix the template over the area to be punched using masking tape and slide a piece of wood underneath. Make indentations by hammering the nail along the outline.

3 Peel the template from the tin to reveal the punched pattern underneath. You can then either leave the tin as it is or pick out details in the pattern using enamel paint. At the back of the punched panel you will notice the tin is quite sharp: tap the hammer over the points gently to knock these back slightly.

Mosaic Planter

Add a splash of colour to your windowsill inside or out.

MATERIALS

wooden planter

pencil

chisel

hammer

emulsion paint

paintbrush

cloth

tile adhesive/grout

coloured tile

strip of cardboard

Hints

Always work away from you when using cutting tools; it is all too easy to slip.

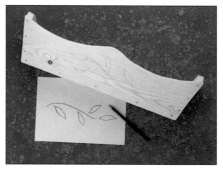

1 Transfer the simple line drawing from this page on to your planter using a pencil. Depending on the size of the planter, you may need to scale this drawing up using a photocopier, or draw your own motif directly on to the planter using this leaf as a guide.

2 Chisel along the outlines of the design using short sharp taps of the hammer to a depth of approximately 6mm/$\frac{1}{4}$ in. Then gouge out the wood inside the outlines using a specialist tool or the chisel. Try to maintain an even depth to the design.

3 Mix an equal quantity of emulsion paint with water and use this to paint the outside of the planter. While the paint is still wet remove some of it with a damp cloth so that the wood grain can still be seen through the painted surface.

4 Smash up the coloured tile between sheets of newspaper (see page 32). Then use the strip of cardboard to push tile adhesive/grout into the groove and press small pieces of the tile into it and allow to dry. Spread a further layer of adhesive/grout over the mosaic, wipe the surface with the damp cloth and leave to dry.

Roller Blind

Most plain bamboo roller blinds can be given this colourful treatment - match the colour to your walls.

MATERIALS

roller blind

emulsion paint

plastic container

paintbrush

fabric

scissors

PVA adhesive

glue brush

needle

thread

Hints

Stretch the blind gently as you paint it to open up the weave so these gaps don't become clogged with paint.

1 Mix together a solution of paint and water using equal quantities of each in the plastic container. Unroll the blind on to sheets of newspaper and pull back the cord to protect it from the splashy paint. Paint the front, leave to dry, and then turn over to paint the back.

2 Cut two strips of fabric to the length of the blind and one strip to the width of the blind. Each strip should be 7.5cm/3in wide. Stitch a small seam down the edges of each strip. Spread glue along the inside of the longer strips, fold in half and cover each edge of the blind with one strip.

3 Spread glue along the inside edge of the smaller strip and fold the ends inwards to make an arrow-shaped point. Fold in half and slip the blind inside the fabric strip as before. The arrow head mitres the fabric, making a neater finish.

4 Use an invisible stitch to secure the fabric binding to the blind. Push the needle through all the thicknesses, pull the thread tight and then pull the needle through to the front again. Continue along all three sides. Reassemble the cords and hang the blind according to the instructions.

Mosaic and Shell Border

Equally at home in the kitchen or the bathroom, this border makes use of broken china and tiles.

MATERIALS

scallop shells	tile adhesive/grout
pencil	broken tiles
Blue-tac	broken china
tape measure	cloth
thin cardboard	spreader

Hints

Using a damp cloth, rub the top layer of adhesive/grout from the surface of the mosaic before it is dry. Otherwise it could take you longer to remove this than it takes to build up the whole border.

1 To make the wave stencil, position the shells along the top of the wall tiles and mark their position with a pencil. Hold them in place with Blue-tac, measure the distance between the shells and transfer on to cardboard. Draw a wave between these measurements and cut out the shape.

2 Remove the shells from the wall and position the wave stencil between the pencil marks. Spread adhesive/grout through the wave stencil maintaining an even thickness. Prepare only two or three waves at a time or the adhesive/grout will have dried before the mosaic pieces are in place.

3 While the adhesive/grout is still wet, push the pieces of broken tiles and china into the surface, building up an intricate mosaic pattern. Move on to the next group of waves as one group is finished. When dry, spread more adhesive/grout on to the tiles, wiping off the excess with a damp cloth.

Harlequin Cupboard

We often cover the surface of shelves, but what about the back of a shelf unit? I think a simple treatment like this looks eye-catching both on open shelves or inside a cupboard.

MATERIALS

tape measure

pencil

ruler

coloured papers

scissors

wallpaper paste

paintbrush

Hints

Don't feel restricted to plain colours for this treatment: two designs of floral wrapping papers would have a pretty patchwork effect. I have used three diamonds along the length of the cupboard, but depending on the length of your shelves you may want fewer or more to cover the space.

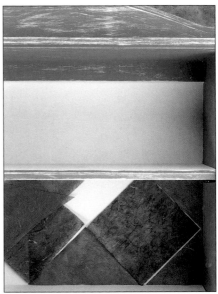

1 To establish the width of the harlequin diamond, measure the length of the area to be covered and divide into three. To determine the height of the diamond, measure the distance between the two shelves. Transfer these measurements to the papers and cut out your diamonds in both colours of paper.

2 Glue the diamonds in place using wallpaper paste. Glue the whole diamonds first, then cut the others into halves and quarters to fill in the gaps. Repeat this procedure for each space until all your shelf back has been covered.

Two-toned Napkins

Use this panelling technique to make a small square of fabric into a large napkin: the more expensive the fabric, the deeper the border should be.

MATERIALS

plain fabric

patterned fabric

iron and ironing board

bias binding

sewing machine

threads (2 colours)

Hints

Choose fabrics that can be washed together and avoid those that are for dry cleaning only.

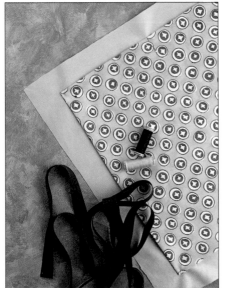

1 Cut the plain fabric to the required size of your napkin (40cm/16in is a generous size), but it could be larger or smaller as you wish. Trim your patterned fabric into a smaller square and turn under the raw edges with a hot iron. Choose a coloured bias binding to complement the fabrics.

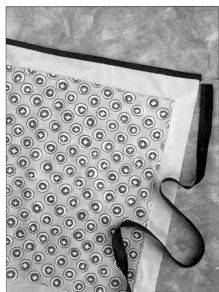

2 Pin the patterned square on to the plain fabric ensuring the borders are even all round. Use a close zigzag machine stitch to sew in place. Stitch the raw edge of the binding to the wrong side of the napkin, turn over to trap the raw edge and sew closed. Use four separate binding pieces for the neatest edging.

Kitchen Wall
Treatment

Colour each photocopy
individually or use a colour
photocopier, either way your
kitchen walls will be far
from boring.

MATERIALS

black-and-white photocopies

scissors

gouache colours

wallpaper paste

paintbrush

Hints

If you can find a vegetable print in a
gardening magazine or catalogue, use this
if you prefer.

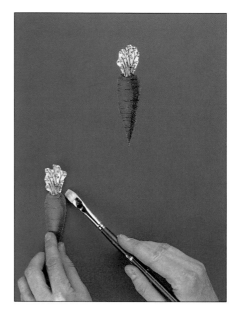

1 Photocopy six individual motifs from
the original on this page, enlarging if
necessary. Then assemble these and place
onto the photocopier so that the next copy
has six motifs printed on it. Colour the
motifs simply using two gouache colours,
then copy this on a colour photocopier until
you have enough motifs to cover the walls.

2 Cut each motif from the copy paper
and paste these on to the wall using
wallpaper paste. Arrange the motifs around
the kitchen fittings as you wish: it is better
if they don't form a regular pattern.

CHAPTER 3

COLOUR CREATIONS

Take inspiration from these terracotta walls and use the plastic bag style of painting to transform your home, using colours to suit your own taste. I've created a strongly coloured finish, but the technique works just as well using softer colours.

If you like the stencilled wall decorations in plaster relief - but not all over the wall - then use one motif spaced regularly at dado height. Be guided by the projects, but find your own solutions for your own home.

If you are planning something on a smaller scale, take the silk flowers out of the vase and sew them into a cushion or a tieback, it's often the surprise of the unfamiliar that catches your eye. Even the more conventional painted glassware is given an exotic touch with the addition of a few glass beads. Nothing could be simpler but the result is stunning.

Covered Footstool

Most footstools are covered in rather boring fabric and although I am using two colours of plain cotton, this method of cutting away one fabric to reveal another underneath is very attractive.

Hints

If possible, remove the legs from the footstool first as this makes fitting the fabric easier.

1 Cut the fabrics to fit over, around and just beneath the footstool. Baste the pieces together. Enlarge the template below on a photocopier to a suitable size. Use it to draw the stars on the top fabric, avoiding the fabric edges. Pin around the stars.

2 Use a contrasting thread and a close zigzag stitch on the sewing machine to stitch around the star outlines. Carefully cut inside the sewn areas on the top layer only.

3 Place the fabric right side down and lay the footstool over this. Pull the fabric over the sides and staple it to the underside of the stool, keeping the fabric taught.

4 Fold the corners to make neat mitred folds. Using tacks, attach a piece of hessian to the underside of the footstool covering the row of staples. Paint the legs to match the top and reassemble.

Sunflower Tiebacks

You could stitch any silk flower on to a tieback, but these
sunflowers really brighten up a room.

MATERIALS

old tieback

hessian or plain fabric

sewing machine

thread

silk flowers

needle

tieback rings

Hints

Re-cover your old tiebacks using hessian or a plain fabric, or stitch the flowers on plain,
ready-made tiebacks.

1 Using the old tieback as a guide, cut the
hessian adding 2.5cm/1in all round for
turning. Turn the allowance over on to the
wrong side, press and then machine stitch
in place.

2 Pull the leaves and flowers from their
plastic stalks and stitch the leaves in
place first, using long stitches. Then stitch
on the sunflower head with as many stitches
as it needs: it will look untidy at the back.

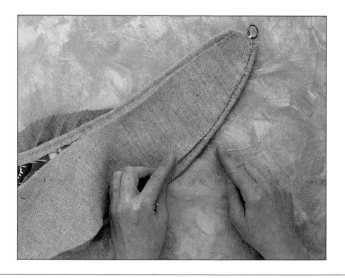

3 Cut another piece
of hessian as
before and press the
allowance under. Sew
this by hand on the
wrong side of the
tieback to hide all the
stitching. Sew two rings
on either end of the
tieback to complete.

Coloured Woodstained Table

Coloured woodstains can be found in many colours in addition to brown mahogany or chestnut, and it is a refreshing change to see them used in this way.

MATERIALS

coffee table

tape measure

masking tape

craft knife

ruler

3 coloured woodstains

saucers

paintbrushes

furniture wax

Hints

Woodstain must always be applied to unfinished wood for the pigment to be absorbed. If you are using an old table, make sure it has been well sanded or stripped before starting. If you have a rectangular table, you may wish to have one long, thin diamond or three smaller ones in the centre.

1 Determine the depth of the border and mark this area with masking tape. Mark the centre of each internal edge along the masking tape and join these marks using more tape to create the centre diamond. Score along the internal edges of all the taped areas with a ruler and craft knife to prevent the stains from bleeding across the grain.

2 Pour a little of the first colour into a saucer and apply this within the masked-off area. The colour quickly seeps into the wood and you can see the grain showing through. Allow the colour to dry for a few minutes before removing the tape.

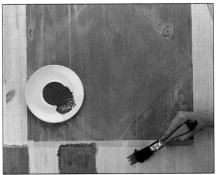

3 Place masking tape across the edges of the diamond you have just painted to protect this colour: the edge of the tape should touch the edge of the stain and the scored line. Paint the resulting four triangular areas with the second woodstain colour.

4 Divide the sides of the border into the even squares that will form the checkerboard effect: ensure you have an uneven number of squares on each side of the border. Mask off every other square and score the table as before and paint on the third colour.

5 Remove the tape once the third colour has had a few minutes to dry; then mask off the painted squares to enable you to paint the final checker squares using the first colour once more. Stain the rest of the table using one colour. Protect with wax if required.

Harlequin Cushion

This really is simpler than the pattern may suggest and looks wonderful in an armchair or on a sofa.

MATERIALS

writing paper

ruler

pencil

scissors

felt (2 colours)

sewing machine

thread

backing cloth

zip

crochet thread

cardboard

needle

Hints

You could cheat and buy ready-made tassels for the corners of this cushion, but the simple homemade variety are easy to make and cost very little.

1 Fold a sheet of writing paper into quarters. Place folded corner to bottom left and make a mark 7.5cm/3in up from the corner on the left edge and another mark 11cm/4 ³/8in along the edge to the right of the corner. Join the marks and cut along the line. Unfold the paper to produce the diamond template. Use this to cut an equal number of green and yellow diamonds.

2 Stitch the edges of alternate coloured diamonds together to produce several long strips. Then sew each strip together along its length, making sure you always place a green diamond next to a yellow one.

3 Trim the strips down two edges to form a corner for your cushion and use the off-cuts to build up the shape of the cushion. Keep turning the fabric over to check that the diamonds are still in line with each other and that their points touch.

4 With right sides together, sew the backing cloth to the felt inserting a zip along one of the shortest sides. Turn right sides out and gently pull the cushion into shape. To make the tassels, wind crochet thread around a piece of cardboard twice the width of the completed tassel length. Slide the threads off and fold in half. Bind the top with thread, then stitch in place.

Punched Tin Hearts Storage Box

Coloured tin shapes are simple to make from aluminium cans and look so attractive that I guarantee you'll be looking for other surfaces to decorate in this way.

MATERIALS

aluminium can

all-purpose scissors

marker pen

piece of wood

nail

hammer

enamel paint

paintbrush

flat headed tacks

Hints

The aluminium may be cut with an old pair of scissors, but don't be tempted to use your best pair unless you want them to be blunted.

1 Trace the outlines from this page enlarging on a photographer if necessary. Cut the top and bottom from the aluminium can and, using the heart template, transfer the outline to the wrong side of the can with the marker pen. Cut out the tin hearts. Protect your hands with gloves at this stage as the tin can be sharp.

2 Place the tin hearts on the wood and punch a series of tiny holes around the edge of the hearts using the nail and hammer. For a pretty effect, keep the holes as close together as possible. I also punched a tiny heart shape inside the larger heart.

3 Decorate some or all of the hearts with a little enamel paint and allow to dry. Then secure each heart to the box using small, flat-headed tacks - I used five tacks around each heart. If the ends of the tacks come through to the other side of the box you will need to file them down.

Gerbera Bowl

This wonderful decoration for a simple papier-mâché bowl was achieved by pressing two gerbera flower heads under a colour photocopier.

MATERIALS

beach ball

newspaper

lining paper

wallpaper paste

scissors

cardboard

white emulsion paint

2 vibrant colours of emulsion paint

gerberas

paper glue

paintbrush

acrylic varnish

Hints

Build up alternate layers of newspaper and lining paper dipped in wallpaper paste over half a beach ball. Allow each layer to dry before applying the next. Once the bowl has about three layers it can be removed from the ball. Use scissors to trim a neat edge around the bowl, making subsequent layers easier to apply. Five layers should be sufficient.

1 Finish the final layer with lining paper and place three wide discs of cardboard underneath the bowl to make a base. Cover the base in the same way, until it is covered and feels quite secure. Allow to dry overnight.

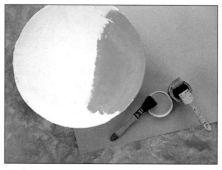

2 Paint the inside and outside of the bowl with two coats of white emulsion paint letting each coat dry before applying the next one. Paint one vibrant shade on the inside and the other on the outside of the bowl. I used acid green on the inside so that my photocopied gerberas would show clearly, and bright orange on the outside of the bowl.

3 Put the gerbera heads directly on the glass of a colour photocopier and make eight copies. Cut around each printed flower carefully and glue to the inside edge of the bowl. When dry, protect with two layers of acrylic varnish.

Verdigris Table Decorations

Verdigris occurs as a natural oxidization process on brass or copper: this reaction can be speeded up with the use of special chemicals, available from good craft shops.

Hints

Once brass or copper has been given a verdigris treatment, it should only be used for decorative purposes.

1 Rub the surfaces to be treated with sandpaper until they become covered with tiny scratches and all the shininess has disappeared. Smaller pieces such as curtain rings can be prepared with emery paper and steel wool.

2 Pour a little of the chemical solution into a saucer and protect your hands with plastic gloves. Dip the paintbrush into the solution and work it into the pitted brass surface. After a few minutes you will start to see a greeny tinge appearing.

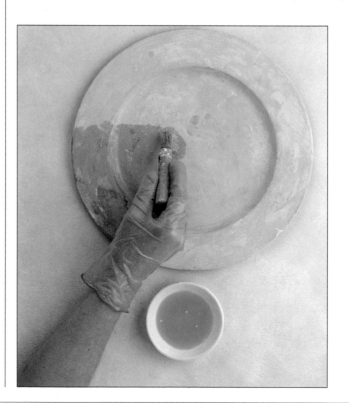

3 After the first coat has dried, apply a second layer of the chemical - this should greatly improve the colour of the verdigris. If necessary, continue applying coats of the solution until the desired patina is achieved.

Studded
Glass Bowl

The glass beads on this glass bowl
are normally used for flower
arrangements but I couldn't resist
decorating the sides of this bowl
with them.

MATERIALS

glass bowl

chinagraph marker pencil

tape measure

self-adhesive plastic

top from glass paint bottle

scissors

glass paint

saucer

stencil brush

glass beads

glass bond glue

Hints

Wait for a sunny day to glue the glass beads
to the bowl as the bonding solution needs
ultraviolet light to work.

1 Using the chinagraph pencil, mark eight points around the top of the bowl: use the tape measure across the centre of the bowl as a guide. Cut eight small discs from the self-adhesive plastic using the top of the glass paint bottle as a template.

2 Peel the backing paper from the plastic discs and position them over the chinagraph marks. Pour a little glass paint into a saucer and dip the ends of the stencil brush in. Paint the outside of the bowl using a stippling motion, spiralling the paint as you work.

3 When the glass paint has dried to the touch, peel off the discs of plastic. The glass paint needs 24 hours to be really dry enough to use and this often depends on how dry or damp the atmosphere is. If in doubt, leave the bowl for several days before use.

4 Glue the beads to the glass - you can do this when the paint is touch dry. Using the glass bond, glue one bead in each circle of clear glass. Adhere the beads near a window to allow the ultraviolet light to set the glue. You can wipe the bowl clean after use but do not put it in a dishwasher.

Silk Flowers Cushion

I think this is a very attractive way to display silk flowers - much better than putting a few plastic stems in a glass vase.

MATERIALS

silk flowers

cushion cover

thread

needle

Hints

I have used small flower heads here, but you could equally well use larger ones. The cushions are most attractive if the heads are sewn closely together.

1 Remove all the tiny flower heads from the plastic stalks and push out any plastic stamens that may be a part of the flower. Choose a cushion cover that harmonizes with the colour of the flowers as they aren't sewn on the back of the cushion.

2 Remove the cushion pad and fold in the four corners of the cushion to meet at the centre. Press the folds, then open up and stitch a row of pink flower heads along the creases, taking care to make the stitches as discreet as possible on the front.

3 Allow the flower heads to overlap slightly as you stitch them to the cover. Work the centre section first, stitching the paler flowers towards the centre. Fill in the four corners with the blue flowers using the same overlapping technique when stitching them in place.

Fabric Padded Picture Frame

You only need a small remnant of a sumptuous raw silk to transform
an old picture frame in this way.

MATERIALS

picture frame	silk fabric
scrap paper	wadding
pencil	PVA adhesive
scissors	glue brush

Hints

Choose a frame that has little or no moulding on the front as these are likely to wrinkle
the fabric when it is stretched across the front of the frame.

1 Separate the glass and back from the
frame. Draw around the inside and
outside edges of the frame on the paper.
Add 5cm/2in borders both inside and
outside the frame and use this as a template
to cut out a piece of fabric. Snip the inside
diagonal corners of the fabric almost up to
the inside frame pencil marks.

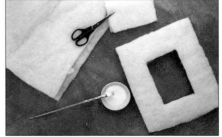

2 Cut a piece of wadding to fit over
the front of the frame. Trim a sliver
of wadding from the inside edge as the
wadding will squash down and cover this
gap when the fabric is pulled over. Glue
the wadding to the frame. I used a double
thickness of wadding to give a more
rounded appearance.

3 Place the frame, face down, on the
wrong side of the fabric, lining up the
diagonal cuts on the inside and making sure
the borders are even all around. Glue along
the inside and outside edges of the frame.
Make sure a little glue is spread to the
back of the frame to hold the fabric securely.
Pull the fabric over the edges and press into
the glue.

4 Mitre the edges carefully to give a neat
finish. If the back of the frame is visible
when displayed, you may wish to cut a
panel of fabric and glue this over the raw
edges. Use the paper template as a pattern
for the fabric. Reassemble the frame,
including your chosen picture.

Plaster Wall Decoration

Mix together coloured emulsion paint with ordinary filler and use a spreader to push the mixture through a simply-cut stencil for a unique wall decoration.

MATERIALS

manila paper

craft knife

pencil

filler

coloured emulsion paint

plastic container

spreader

double-sided tape

Hints

You could use thin cardboard for your stencil rather than manila paper, but paint it with two layers of oil-based paint first so that it doesn't go soggy.

1 Enlarge the templates from this page to an appropriate size. Trace the designs on to the manila paper and use the craft knife to cut out the shapes carefully. You will need to leave a border of at least 7.5cm/3in around the stencil.

2 Mix together enough emulsion paint and filler to make a thick but spreadable paste. If necessary, add a little water although I tend to find that most emulsion paints contain enough water. Mix thoroughly with the spreader to remove any lumps.

Living Room Wall Treatment

Strange as it may seem, this paint finish has been achieved using a plastic bag rather than a paintbrush. Thin washes of colour have been layered on top until the desired effect is reached.

MATERIALS

yellow emulsion paint

terracotta emulsion paint (2 shades)

paintbrushes

plastic bags

plastic container

mixing brush

Hints

This is a paint finish that definitely improves as more and more layers are added so don't be discouraged at the start - I warn you, the surface does look a bit messy!

1 Prepare the surfaces to be painted, then cover the floor and furniture. Start by applying wide splodges of both colours with a large paintbrush. I have used one shade of yellow and two of terracotta for this paint treatment. Work one area at a time, say one whole wall, then move around the room.

2 While the paint is still wet, press a crumpled plastic bag on to the wet surface and then lift if off and press into another area of wet paint. Continue all over the wet paint area, then repeat the process. You will need to replace each bag as it becomes saturated with paint.

3 Use pieces of double-sided tape to temporarily fix the stencil on the wall. Using the spreader, scrape the filler over the surface of the stencil. Don't overload the spreader or you may find the filler moving behind the stencil and spoiling the motif. Peel back the stencil and leave to dry.

3 Dilute one shade of terracotta with an equal quantity of water in a plastic container and mix together to produce a thin solution of paint. Apply this using a large brush to the surface of the 'bagged' paint using broad loose strokes as if you were cleaning the wall. Build some areas up using three or four washes like this and leave others with only one wash.

CHAPTER 4

COLOUR BY DESIGN

If, like me, you're always keeping one eye out for ideas, and the other one on the decorating budget, then you can't go wrong with many of the ideas in this chapter. My stylish curtain banner makes economical use of expensive fabrics yet produces a stunning window display. The largest amount of fabric you will need for any one curtain is half the drop as you simply cut the fabric in half lengthways and then sew the two halves together, end to end. Follow my instructions for the curtain trimming to edge the banner, then dye muslin for the backing and sew together. It couldn't be easier and not only do you have a stunning look for your windows, it literally halves your fabric costs. Try my colour transformations on hat boxes, mirror frames, chairs and stencilled walls and you could even find yourself piping coloured filler on to your picture frames!

Stencilled Floorcloth

I love these simple, hard-wearing cloths because you can decorate them in whatever pattern or style you fancy. Let the children decorate their own bedroom cloth, covering the floor with lots of newspaper first. All you need to do is let the paint dry, then protect it with acrylic varnish.

MATERIALS

canvas

scissors

sewing machine

thread

cloth

iron and ironing board

pencil

ruler

emulsion paints

paintbrush

manila paper

craft knife

double-sided tape

stencil brush

Hints

For a completely no-sew project, you can glue the hems down using PVA adhesive.

1 Cut the canvas to the size of cloth you require plus 5cm/2in all around for the hem. Turn the hem under, machine stitch and then press down firmly with a damp cloth and a hot iron. Fold the corners over neatly to avoid any large bumps that will show on the other side.

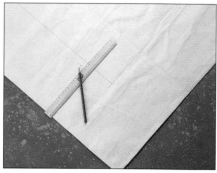

2 Draw a deep border around all four sides using a pencil and ruler (keep the pencil line as faint as possible). My 122cm/48in cloth has a border of 20cm/8in. Spread lots of newspaper under the cloth prior to painting.

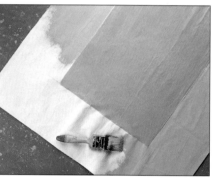

3 Paint in the central area first using two coats of a bright emulsion paint. Brush the paint up to the drawn line but don't despair too much if your line is a little wobbly, it all adds to the character of the cloth. Paint the border using two coats. Allow to dry thoroughly.

4 Enlarge the tulip outline on this page to a suitable size on a photocopier and transfer it on to a piece of manila paper. Cut around the outline carefully using a craft knife. (Thin cardboard will do if you first cut out the design and protect the cardboard with two layers of oil-based paint.)

5 Place small pieces of double-sided tape underneath the stencil and lay the stencil on the border. Stencil tulips using coloured emulsion or acrylic paints, angling one into each corner. Measure the distance between each corner stencil and space more tulips evenly between.

Scrolled
Picture Frame

Although it's not edible, decorating
this frame is just like icing a cake.

MATERIALS

coloured emulsion paint

filler

plastic container

mixing brush

thick paper

sticky tape

scissors

frame

Hints

There's no need to be confined to scrolls
when decorating your picture frames: pipe
the filler into zigzags or circles, even straight
lines look just as good.

1 Mix equal quantities of paint and filler in the plastic container, adding a little more of either until you have made a thick paste; it will take a few minutes of stirring to get rid of any lumps. Twist a square of paper into a cone and secure it with sticky tape.

2 Drop the paint filler mixture into the cone with a teaspoon and roll the top down as you would an ordinary piping bag. Snip off the end of the cone and pipe the decoration on to the frame. Keep on piping the mixture until the frame is covered entirely, and leave it to dry before reassembling.

Hat Boxes

A tower of these boxes looks
attractive as well as providing
valuable storage space in
a bedroom.

MATERIALS

hat boxes
coloured emulsion paints
paintbrush
copyright-free print borders
scissors
PVA adhesive
glue brush
saucer
cloth

Hints

Black-and-white copyright-free books
provide a wealth of source material for lots
of craft ideas, including this one.

1 Paint the hat boxes using toning emulsion paints - I used these pretty ice cream colours, but strong primaries would work just as well. Photocopy the page of border designs until you have enough of each design to wrap around a hatbox. Cut out each border.

2 Glue each border section around the edge of the hat boxes, using your fingers to smooth each section down to remove any small air bubbles. Butt the ends up to each other carefully as any overlaps will spoil the border.

3 Mix together a little of the base colour emulsion paint with an equal quantity of water and brush this quickly over the paper border. Wipe a cloth over the surface of the paint before it has had a chance to dry, removing more paint from the printed areas and less from the cut edge. Leave to dry.

Painted Chair

Junk shops are great places for finding good quality, sturdy chairs such as this one, and with the minimum of preparation and a quick paint finish they are totally transformed.

MATERIALS

chair

sandpaper (medium grade)

wood mouldings

wood glue

glue brush

2 colours of emulsion paint

paintbrush

Hints

If you can find old chairs in junk shops, it would cost very little to have a complete set of chairs decorated in this way.

1 Prepare the surface of the chair for painting. If your chair is varnished as mine was, sandpaper is all you need to use for a smooth finish. Use wood glue to glue the mouldings in place. Leave the glue to dry thoroughly before starting to paint.

2 Paint the first emulsion layer on the chair and allow this to dry thoroughly before painting on the second colour. Distressing colour in this way is always more successful if the darkest paint is applied last.

3 Use the sandpaper to wear away some of the second colour to reveal the first colour underneath. If you accidentally remove too much paint so that you can see the wood itself, simply use a little of the top-colour emulsion to paint this in.

Chair Seat Cover

This chair has a drop-in seat which is perfect for this checkerboard cover made from two colours of inexpensive cotton fabric.

MATERIALS

seat base

2 colours of cotton fabric

scissors

sewing machine

thread

staple gun

Hints

Once made, protect the chair covers with spray-on fabric guard which repels everyday spills and splashes.

1 Cut the fabric into 7.5cm/3in-wide strips. The strips must be long enough to cover the seat base and turn to the underside where they will be stapled. Make two panels, each consisting of four strips machine sewn together. Cut one panel into 7.5cm/3in pieces.

2 Sew three cut-off pieces of fabric together along the narrow edges to make a long strip and repeat. Sew the two resulting strips together along their length to form a checker pattern. Stitch this along the edge of the central panel. Sew together another checker panel and stitch this along the other side.

3 Trim the fabric to fit the seat base, press. Lay the seat base on the wrong side of the fabric, pull the edges over on to the wooden frame and staple in place. Staple the centre of each edge and work outwards to the corners. Fold the corners neatly and drop the seat into the frame of the chair.

Seashell Cabinet

This cabinet can be hung on the wall or placed on a surface to be used as a glass-lidded display box for pretty soaps and bathroom accessories.

MATERIALS

bathroom cabinet

sandpaper (medium and fine grades)

thin cardboard

pencil

scissors

masking fluid

fine paintbrush

coloured emulsion paints

paintbrush

acrylic varnish

Hints

Paint starfish or fishes on this box as an alternative to these pink scallop shells.

1 Remove any old layers of paint or varnish if you are recycling an old cabinet. Transfer the shell on this page on to thin cardboard and cut along the outline carefully to make a simple stencil. Place the stencil on the cabinet and hold in place. Paint masking fluid between the shell outline and allow to dry.

2 Paint the base colour emulsion over the cabinet; for a more interesting effect, brush the colour on patchily. When the emulsion paint is quite dry, rub the surface of the masking fluid with your finger to start the peeling process, then peel it away to reveal the bare wood. Rub the surface lightly with sandpaper.

3 Paint the scallop shells using patchy areas of pink colour - don't worry if some of the raw wood shows through. When this is dry, add the fine shell details using a fine paintbrush. Seal and protect the cabinet with two layers of acrylic varnish.

Curtain Trimmings

Homemade trimmings are so simple to make you'll wonder why you never made them before.

MATERIALS

coloured canvas

sewing machine

thread

scissors

Hints

Use a contrasting thread for the best effect. If you can't find a colour of canvas to suit your requirements, you could dye natural canvas in a washing machine.

1 Cut long 7.5cm/3in-wide strips of canvas. Fray the edges by teasing the threads open in the weave, then pull them down through the length of the fabric. Fray each strip to a depth of 2.5cm/1in.

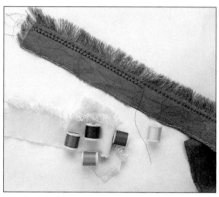

2 Set your sewing machine to an embroidery stitch, if it has one, or a close zigzag if it doesn't. Use contrasting thread. Sew two lines of stitches along the length of each strip, keeping the lines as close to each other as you can.

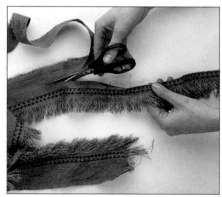

3 Sew the strips together to make lengths as long as you require. Press the seams open and trim the raw edge along the length. Turn this edge under, then stitch the trimming on to your furnishings, keeping the stitching line as close to the folded edge as possible.

Curtain Banner

Tight budgets needn't mean scrimping on beautiful fabrics. This curtain uses two half-widths of fabric and yet still gives the impression of a full curtain.

MATERIALS

patterned fabric	trimming fabric for ties
iron and ironing board	string
sewing machine	needle
thread	muslin
scissors	fabric dye

Hints

Measure the curtain drop, add 5cm/2in for seam allowances and the allowance required for pattern matching, then halve the measurement - giving you the length for your patterned fabric.

1 Cut the selvages from the edges of the fabric and fold the fabric in half down the length. Press, then cut the fabric into two halves. Sew the two halves of fabric together across the width, matching the pattern if necessary. Press this seam open.

2 Turn over the upper and lower hems and sew the trimming down the sides of the fabric, keeping the line of stitching close to the edge of the fabric. Make sure the raw fabric edge is not visible behind the fringe when viewed from the front.

3 To make the curtain ring ties, cut strips measuring 7.5 x 38cm/3 x 15in from the fabric. Fold them in half enclosing a piece of string in one end. Sew across the width, trapping the string in the stitches, and then down the length. Pull the end of the string to draw the tie through to the right side, and sew the end closed.

4 Calculate the amount of muslin you need to cover the window: allow one and-a-half times the width of the frame plus 5cm/2in hem all round. Dye the muslin, dry, then press. Stitch the hems and sew the panel centrally on the muslin. Stitch the ties across the width of the curtain and tie to the curtain pole.

Sink Cabinet

This cabinet has a real beachcomber look, even the handles are made from pieces of driftwood.

MATERIALS

cabinet

white acrylic primer

2 colours of emulsion paint

paintbrush

sandpaper (coarse and medium grades)

Hints

Choose colours that are close in tone for this cabinet and wear the colours away as little or as much as you like - continually assess the distressing process as you work.

1 Paint the cabinet with the white acrylic primer and allow to dry. Make sure all the wood is covered well as the humid conditions in a bathroom are not very kind to wooden furniture.

2 Loosely brush on coats of coloured emulsion paint, layering one coat on top of another but allowing one coat to dry before applying the next. Don't worry about trying to achieve an even layer of colour.

3 Sand the whole cabinet down using first coarse then medium grade sandpaper, controlling the amount of paint removal as you work.

4 Screw a handle in place, or use a piece of driftwood if you prefer.

Mirror Frame

Cut your own frame from a piece
of plywood using a small fret saw.

MATERIALS

frame

coloured emulsion paint

paintbrush

mirror tile

self-adhesive pads

aluminium cans

tin snips

nail

enamel paint

fine paintbrush

hammer

piece of wood

tacks

picture fasteners

Hints

Use gloves to protect your hands as you cut
open the cans because they can be very
sharp. Cut your frame into any shape you
like - my crown is quite dramatic, you may
prefer a heart or diamond, or a regular
square. The only consideration is that the
mirror tile should fit inside the shape with
a narrow border around the sides.

1 Paint the frame and stick the mirror tile in place with the self-adhesive pads aligning it centrally within the frame. Cut the tops and bottoms from the cans and cut a seam down the middle to flatten each one. Trim away any sharp edges.

2 Lay the flattened sheets over the frame and cut the metal into shaped pieces that will fit within the edges of the frame. You may need to use different sections of metal to cover the frame, these should overlap if possible. If you have an unusual shape, like this crown, mark the metal before cutting.

3 When each piece of metal is cut, use the nail to scratch in star and coil shapes on the wrong side. Press hard so that the outlines show through on the right side. Paint the different sections with the enamel paint and allow to dry.

4 Punch a line of decorative holes along the outside edges of each metal section using the nail and hammer. You will find it quicker and easier to punch along a piece of wood - any small piece of scrap wood will do.

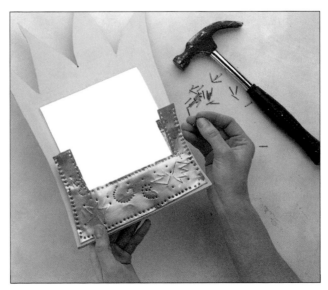

5 Attach the metal pieces to the frame with small tacks. Use several tacks around the corners and angles to make sure that these edges do not lift up and scratch. Attach picture fasteners to the back of the frame to hang it on a wall.

Star Lampshade

When the light is switched on, the stars illuminate the delicate tissue paper.

MATERIALS

thin paper

pencil

lampshade

craft knife

2 colours of emulsion or water-based paint

paintbrush

tissue paper

paper/fabric adhesive

glue brush

Hints

If you have acrylic or gouache water-based colours, use these rather than the emulsion colours. However, you will need to apply the base colour thickly to achieve an opaque finish. The second colour needs to be diluted to splatter successfully.

1 Lay the thin paper over the star motifs on this page and draw around their edges using a pencil. Press the paper to the inside of the lampshade until you can see the outlines of the stars showing through. Draw these star shapes randomly over the lampshade.

2 Cut around the drawn pencil outlines on the shade using a sharp craft knife. Always work with the blade away from you and cut through the fabric shade slowly and carefully. Paint the shade using the base colour. Allow to dry, then splatter the thinner, second colour over the first to create a speckled finish.

3 For each of the stars, tear a piece of tissue paper slightly larger than the outlines and glue to the inside of the frame using adhesive. Before the adhesive is dry, use the craft knife to cut the excess tissue paper at the back of the shade into star shapes. When the light is switched on, these outlines will be visible through the shade.

Bedroom Wall Treatment

A simple motif such as this one is easy to cut if you follow these steps. If your stencil is to follow a regular pattern, measure out and mark a grid of squares on the walls using a tape measure and place the stencil in the centre of each square. Alternatively, place the stencil on the walls at random.

MATERIALS

pencil

manila paper

craft knife

double-sided tape

gold acrylic paint

stencil brush

Hints

If you cannot find manila paper, use thin cardboard. First cut your stencil, then paint the cardboard with two layers of oil-based paint and leave to dry before stencilling. The paint prevents the cardboard from becoming soggy.

1 Use a photocopier to enlarge the size of the motif on this page and transfer the image on to the manila paper. Cut around the outline using a sharp craft knife.

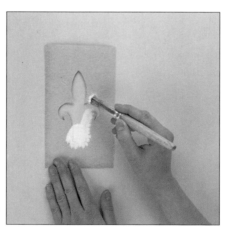

2 Hold the stencil in place with double-sided tape. Dip the stencil brush into the paint, dab off the excess and then apply the paint using a stippling motion with the brush. Peel off the stencil and repeat.

ACKNOWLEDGMENTS

The publishers would like to thank the following companies for providing the merchandise used in our photographs.

Accessories The Pier, 200 Tottenham Court Road, London W1P 0AD
The General Trading Company, 144 Sloane Street, Sloane Square, London SW1

Paints Dulux ICI Paints, Wexham Road, Slough, Berks (Customer Advice Tel: 0753 550555)

Woodcraft Products Somerset Creative Products, Charlecot, Mark Causeway, Mark, Somerset TA9 4PX

GLOSSARY

US readers may not be familiar with the following terms:

UK	US
aluminium	aluminum
Bondaweb	fusible webbing
biscuit tin	cookie tin
car boot sale	yard or garage sale
chinagraph pencil	chinagraph marker
curtain rail	curtain rod or track
emulsion paint	latex paint
fret saw	scroll saw
hardboard	masonite
hessian	burlap
junk shop	secondhand store or thrift shop
lining paper	plain shelf paper
matt	matte or flat finish
mount (for pictures)	mat
muslin	cheesecloth
notice board	bulletin board
noughts and crosses	tic-tac-toe
panel pins	brads
PVA adhesive	white or yellow craft glue
roller blind	window shade
rubbish	trash, garbage
wadding	batting
zip	zipper